I0011392

Blender Meets Python Vol. 1:

Blender 2.6 Unites with Python 3 for a

Completely 3D Relationship

Authored By

Jordan Kaufman

Justin Valencia

i

ISBN: 1490351124
ISBN-13: 978-1490351124

DEDICATION

For me, this book is dedicated
to my father, Dean Valencia,
who taught me the meaning
of a true work ethic.

Justin

For my part I dedicate this book to my mother,
Priscilla Iris Kaufman,
who let her 16 year old son move to Europe
to seize an opportunity during the tech boom.

Jordan

CONTENTS

ACKNOWLEDGMENTS

Front Cover Photo Art: **Ritchie Hamilton**
Concept Artist: **Elijah LaMarca**
Editing and Forward: **Jordan Kaufman**
Copy Consultant: **Elliot I.K.**
Proof Readers: **Jamie M.K.** and **Anonymous**

Chess Board: **Nathan**
(could not get a last name, but his work speaks for itself)
http://**www.blender-models.com/**model-
downloads/objects/id/chessboard/

Snipt
*(yes we thank abstract entities in this book, in this case
for providing a great platform to make code available,
including **all of the examples** found in this book)*:
https://snipt.net/BlenderMeetsPython/

Blender Foundation: for obvious reasons
Python Software Foundation: by now, painfully obvious reasons.

FORWARD

When asked to provide a forward for this volume, I immediately accepted on two grounds: First, with the plethora of books written on Python Scripting, and the cache of great Blender 3D books each remaining in their separate universes, it was long overdue to publish a book that quickly and elegantly laid out how to bring Python Scripting to Blender 3D.

Secondly, in the years I've known Justin, I have seen him repeatedly pick up new technologies quickly and methodically with a contagious excitement that is more rare than it should be.

Also, I was there when he first set his eyes on Blender, and when he took on the huge task of having to learn Blender and Python over a holiday weekend so that our firm could take on a project for a local film studio that we almost passed up, since we were swamped with other work and had no in-house Python competency at the time. I will be eternally grateful to him for this, since it allowed us to form a partnership with said studio, namely Fulcrum Films, that is poised to change the nature of the work we do at Level Development from being purely about code development solutions, to becoming a cutting edge agile animation development house (for more on this you can jump to Chapter 8 that I also wrote, and sort of acts like an afterword about what we are doing and how we need your help).

This may be our first book on technology, but it will not be our last. Anyone that has had the pleasure of working with Justin picks up immediately that he is young, hungry, smart, and extremely motivated. That quality certainly rubs off, so I am sure he will get us working on Volume 2 in no time. He learns extremely quickly and in this small book, he makes it easy for you to do so as well. It is as if he not only learns quickly, but understands why most people struggle. Because of this, he lays out the material so logically that it's hard not to immediately pick up what is being taught. It has been my pleasure to work with him on this volume and help with smoothing out some of the rough edges, along with providing some (hopefully) inspiring words in Chapter 8 that we agreed I should write, to promote the firm and our mission that I think you will find worth reading.

While working at Level Development, Justin learned SQL Server faster than I've ever seen. I remember exclaiming, "He'd never heard of relational databases a month ago and now he knows T-SQL in and out!"

Obviously, when he started at our firm his career was just beginning, but he wasn't "green" for long. I hope you find it as much of a pleasure to learn from him as it was to work with him!

I do expect in the coming years to find many more books following the trail blazed by this little volume. In keeping with the tradition of open source development the cost of this book has been kept low so that anyone interested can get it in some format. I know I can speak for both of us when I say that money was not even close to the main motivator in putting this work together. Valencia is just getting started and I applaud his Primus Opus (which I'm sure he would modestly call "our Primus Opus") and am confident you will enjoy it as well, especially if you are among the exclusive (read: tiny) subset of the population that not only wants to make use of the powerful Blender 3D creation suite, but also wants to expand its reach through Python 3 scripting (you must love learning curves and the massive rewards that await on the other end of the rainbow).

Well, that was a mouthful, but the rest of this book promises to be concise and get right to the point, so you can be up and running with your first Python/Blender script in just a few short hours.

Jordan Robert Kaufman
@Jordan_RK

QUESTIONS: WHO SHOULD READ AND WHAT VERSION?

There are two important questions we should get right out of the way.

WHO SHOULD READ THIS BOOK?

If you have already successfully written and ran python scripts within Blender, then I believe you will find this book too introductory and basic. We still think you should buy this book, of course (since we are so biased), to support our work and then give it to someone who is not so Blender/Python savvy.

Before you pass this volume along, however, please make sure to read "**Chapter 8** – I Have Been To The Model Top" which is like our "mission statement" from Jerry Maguire (only it isn't insanely directing our organization to earn less money by taking fewer clients) so if you are into revolutionizing the world of Projected Animation, you will enjoy it.

ONE VERSION OF THE SAME STORY

All the examples were executed within **Blender 3D version 2.66** (even though 2.66a was just released – shame on us I know).

As far as Python the examples adhere to **Python 3** (since that is what is used within Blender 2.66 it does make some kind of sense).

If you have any other versioning questions just contact us at: **filmfulcrum@gmail.com**

3

INTRO: THIS BOOK AND THE OPEN SOURCE MOVEMENT

My first thought was to name this book **"Snake Smoothies"** and have the front cover picture the python actually in the blender, but I thought that might be a little too hostile. Then I thought **"Blender and Python: A Love Story",** but I didn't want my book to be incorrectly associated to the latest Michael Moore film. So I settled on "Blender Meets Python", the story of how an open teenage 3D modeling suite coming of age meets a slightly older, stable but open-minded, scripting language named Python.

Like most great romances, they get along great, each of them bringing out the best in each other. Blender is beautiful and elegant with an understated power lurking beneath. In spite of being a little older, Python is always up for anything, yet he seems to have a deep complexity that would take a lifetime to fully grasp.

While the bond grows deeper with each passing release, their bond can never be exclusive, because every one of these stories needs someone trying to obstruct true eternal love. In this case the culprit is the fan favorite nemesis: the GNU General Public License (infamously known on the street as the GPL).

In actuality, the GPL is a fantastic thing that we will get into later, but I could not help but use this opener (and I will try as I write to refer to Blender in the feminine tense and Python in the masculine tense). I hope by this you can tell how excited I am to put this book together and share it with you. When I first got introduced to Blender I could not believe her power and breadth of functionality (and it was freely available). When I started extending it with Python I was impressed with how comfortable yet powerful the language was and he would regularly show me little surprises (like Duck Typing, which you too will come to love).

I am confident you will get something out of reading this volume and learning how to extend Blender with Python. I am hungry for feedback so please feel free to contact me (iwmsconsultant@gmail.com).

Now is a good time to get into what the open source movement is, and how the GPL (and similar licenses) play a part for those new to the concept. All others please skip along to the chapter that you deem is a good starting point for your level of previous exposure.

THE OPEN SOURCE MOVEMENT

I do not intend to provide a complete history of the Open Source movement (since you can easily get this online), but rather briefly explain what it is and point out a few overlooked areas.

The idea with Open Source is of **"free" software as in "free speech"** (but not necessarily like "free beer"). In general you can still sell your software or operating system, but you can't infringe on the right of the purchaser/receiver to pass it along or make changes to the source code. Although, you can get them to change the name if you feel the differences are so great that it is warranted, and you can control the use of your logo if you are the originator of the software package in question.

In most software companies, source code is kept closed and guarded. My co-author has even been in a meeting where source code was brought locked in a brief case that was literally handcuffed to a member of a security detail accompanying the software vendor they were meeting with.

As a result, if you don't like something about how MS Word works, I guess you could try and write a macro (yikes!) but you can't simply make changes to the source and recompile because it is under a proprietary license, rather than an Open Source one that would bestow much more freedom to the end user (and much less of a division between the developers and users).

The GPL, (or GNU GPL) we mentioned earlier was created by Richard Stallman and is really what kicked off (or at least solidified) the Open Source movement. GNU was an operating system that preceded Linux (and which recursively stands for "GNU's Not Unix") and was released under the GPL, giving users the non-exclusive right to the source code, the right to make changes and add on features, and to distribute freely (with some very reasonable guidelines spelled out in the GPL).

The beauty of this was not simply the "free" operating system, but that anything that was added would also be under the GPL license. This provision is what keeps the Open Source movement going because in order to get the benefit of all the open source code, you need to agree to keep your additions open source in most cases. This is like a wonderful recursive loop that sees a massive amount of good, usable, and open source software added each year to an already gigantic ocean of awesomeness.

The good news is that Open Source software can almost always be used for commercial purposes, and it does not corrupt your intellectual property rights (DISCLAIMER: this is not meant to be legal counsel in any way – please consult a legal professional as this book contains no legal advice whatsoever). So if you make a 3D movie with Blender you are not compromising your rights to that movie (although many choose to release their models, effects and animation for others to use freely – see the store at Blender3D.org for many low cost options).

Also good news is the fact that there are plenty of ways to make money through Open Sourced software. The first major companies to crop up were companies that offered to support or extend Open Source software for a price (often software they themselves developed and distributed for free to create the market) and companies that sold distributions of Linux with tons of useful software combined. Today many developers get paid to expand Open Source software for specific companies, for those company's internal use. Of course if they choose to distribute their enhancements to other companies (for a fee or gratis), they must make the source code available as well, and confer on the user the right to change and redistribute the delivered code (in most cases). Of course when all else fails, you can always ask for donations to support your Open Source work (while we are on the topic, if you want to support our work you can do so in a very cool and open source way by sending us some fraction of a Bitcoin to the following Bitcoin address:

1KTHCCp6vctHJkSq7EQVVt8DhivnByjBc6).

As a side note, today there are many Open Source licenses besides the GPL, such as MIT's license that Bitcoin uses, which we will get into later.

PAID SOFTWARE IS NOT SYNONOMOUS WITH BETTER

Some think that because most Open Source software is not only free as in "free speech", but also as in "free beer", that it must somehow be categorically inferior. Nothing could be further from the truth.

Don't get me wrong, part of my living involves developing closed sourced software that will not be free in any sense, and there is definitely a place for that. But if you look past the whole issue of cost, you will see that there is a much more important differentiator than price, namely development models.

Proprietary (or Closed Source) software has a development cycle that goes something like this: the initial product is development by a development team and is released; bugs and enhancement requests are submitted to the software vendor and bug reports go to Support to fix, and enhancement requests generally get compiled by an Internal Marketing ("internal" as in information is flowing from the market into the company) department and are given a priority ranking usually based on the quantity of similar requests. Enhancement requests from the market are balanced by the demands of the Sales force and External Marketing, whose responsibility it is to wow the market enough to either buy the software, or plunk down some change for an upgrade. Internal and External marketing fight it out (and sometimes Support will beg for some overarching changes to make their job easier), and eventually the desired changes make it to product development and the cycle repeats.

This approach has many inherent advantages and disadvantages. Right off the bat, you have a compartmentalization of the user, support, and development. Also, what will get someone to buy something (bells and whistles) is not always the same thing that will give them the most value (ease of use, stability, etc). Sometimes this approach does produce better software, especially when the software is being marketed to developers. For example, while I love that MySQL exists and is free to all Apache-loving people to use, I wouldn't put it up against SQL Server 2012 or the latest Oracle release in terms of ease of use, shortened learning curve, or available documentation. That said, when it comes to web servers this doesn't seem to apply as much. I have enjoyed using Apache (Free and Open Source) much more than having to deal with IIS (Microsoft's offering). It has such an elegant simplicity and has everything you really need. Not to mention its efficient use of resources and stability. I am of course not alone in this sentiment and in fact

Apache holds, as of the close of 2012, almost two thirds of the market share among web servers.

With Open Source development often the user is the same person to fix the bugs they find; similarly the end user can end up being user, product marketer, and developer in the case of enhancements. As a result, there may be less flashy bells and whistles in the Open Source world, but what really matters to end users seems to get addressed much more quickly. What actually bothers users on a day to day basis (rather than what looks impressive in a sales presentation) is put at the top of the list, because it has to bother them enough to actually put the time in to code the fix or enhancement. That said, there are plenty of mature Open Source projects with plenty of bells, whistles, and what not to accompany the stability and flexibility common in the Open Source world.

Also, another side benefit of Open Source is that it encourages software development in general. Let's say you don't work in software or you are too young to start working in the corporate world. Without Open Source projects, coding enthusiasts would be relegated to developing their own programs from scratch. This may have been cool at one time, but by today's standards software developed completely by one person is bound to be pretty lame. For example imagine if you had to code, from scratch, a 3D modeling and animation suite like Blender 3D! That would take a lifetime's worth of spare time, and you would never get there. Instead you have access to the source code and can get in there and simply code the functionality you wish was there. Not only that, but you can contribute your work to a community of grateful users and connect with other like-minded coders. The possibilities are endless, and in this volume you will get an introduction to extending Blender 3D with Python, and on how to share that with the Open Source community at large.

Both development models have merit. Proprietary software generally is a little slicker and flashier, and at times this translates into better software. Open Source software provides incredible versatility, so that even small businesses can have powerful yet tailored solutions that would not have been otherwise possible.

As a general rule of thumb I would say: "THINK OPEN SOURCE FIRST!" and if you absolutely have to, use the proprietary option. For those curious, I wrote this book in MS Word 2010 and while that is indeed my preferred word processor, I can't help at laugh every time it freezes to Auto-Save since Lightworks (which is not technically open source but is a free video editing NLE) saves every change immediately without the user ever noticing, and Lightworks handles much more complex operations than text manipulation.

At the time of writing this book, the list of open source end user software applications, enterprise offerings, operating systems, servers, utilities and integrated development environments is truly staggering. Even so, the power of Open Source doesn't stop there.

NOT JUST SOFTWARE!

It's important to note that this Open Source concept stretches beyond just software applications and operating systems in a manner of speaking. For example, there is a similar license for **free documentation** called GNU FDL. I'm sure that doesn't blow your mind, but it is still cool.

Much more exciting is **how we now have Open Source crypto-currency, such as Bitcoin,** where there is no central authority but the integrity of the record keeping is distributed over the network, (which can be viewed as much more difficult to corrupt or control). In this case the Open Source concept has allowed a functioning monetary system develop that no one actually controls… it will hit you a few days from now if that doesn't impress you yet.

Also leaping **out of the digital realm and into our physical reality** we have 3D physical objects entering the Open Source arena. Sites like defcad.org offer free 3D model's that are meant to be printed using a wide array of 3D printers which are rapidly dropping in cost and increasing in quality. You can likely imagine a future when instead of cursing IKEA in frustration for shorting you two bolt H's that you simply download the model for that part online, set copies count to two and hit print! On this front there is even an Open Source 3D Printer (meaning the instructions for the printer are even released and not proprietary) that can replicate itself and is **meant to work with Blender!!!** Check out tantillus.org if you think that is as cool as I do. Tantillus was actually developed on Blender and was originally made with other Open Source 3D printers, but of course can now make itself.

In addition there is an **open source culture** that surrounds all of this that encourages collaboration and fosters the development of some unique work that simply would never have existed at any price. And when choosing an open source tool, it is more than just a cold calculation that it can get the job done at no or little cost. Rather, the more you use open source tools, you will find yourself developing a love for them, and at times will find yourself using an Open Source tool when there is an affordable Proprietary alternative that might even be a little better on paper. But this does make sense, because people who are Open Source conscience tend to use the same tools, so it also functions as a lingua franca. In the making of this book the only proprietary software used was MS Word. The code examples were made using Notepad++, for example, which I highly recommend as an IDE alternative (when you don't need auto complete or to compile code right from your editor).

CHAPTER ONE – BLENDER 3D: WHAT AND WHY

If you are searching out a volume for Blender 3D and Python, then you are likely not new to Blender. Even so, it seems appropriate to include a brief explanation and answer the "what" and "why" of Blender (*just in case a programmer house guest picks up your copy of this book in the middle of the night they won't have so many questions over breakfast*).

As you have likely already gathered, Blender 3D is a powerful Open Source 3D everything machine! It's pretty much a one stop shop where you can do 3D Modeling, Animation, Special Affects, and even develop some serious games.

One thing that often gets overlooked is the fact that video games are really a subset of a larger category, namely of interactive 3D applications; we don't normally think of it in those terms because we don't see many interactive 3D applications used for anything but gaming but that need not limit our imaginations. When e-commerce first became a household name many companies tried to develop 3D malls for people to shop. Obviously these largely (or completely) failed and most, if not all, people didn't do their online shopping in a 3D environment. So far, 3D animation has only proved worthwhile in creating a fantasy environment, either for gaming or for films, but this is changing. Many medical applications are using 3D modeling to analyze genes or viruses, as are architectural programs, fabrication applications (such as used in 3D printing or pre-cast production), and the list goes on.

Obviously acquiring the skills needed to work with 3D computer graphics can be very useful, but choosing a suite to sink your teeth into can be difficult. There are many vendors out there trying to get the attention of graphic artists and developers alike. A glance of wikipedia's list of 3D packages could leave you scratching your head: http://en.wikipedia.org/wiki/3D_computer_graphics_software

That said, if you focus on the section entitled "Open Source (Free) packages" you will see only a half dozen or less packages (five at the time of this printing). Among this group, Blender 3D is the clear champion. Besides being ported to any OS you care about, it is feature rich, powerful, fairly stable, and has a great community of contributors to recommend it.

Even though blender is distributed free of charge it is extremely full featured. In fact the complaint, if any, about Blender is never about it being unable to accomplish something; if anything the complaint centers around the steep learning curve involved. Remember, this is a professional suite of software, so there is no reason to think it will work as easily as an android special video effects app (which may work easily but is very limited in the scope of applications it is capable of).

When I picked up Blender, it made sense to me that if I am going to pick up a 3D graphics suite, I might as well put the time into learning on a platform that's only limitation is my own knowledge. Again, if you are picking up a volume on extending Blender with Python scripting, you have probably already made up your mind, but just in case here is some food for thought:

1. Blender is a one-stop-shop full featured suite. No need to use a separate program for modeling, animation, special effects or game development. The implications to this are huge. Just think of putting out some 3D content (movie, webisode/micro-film, tv show, etc) and how seamlessly you could move into developing the accompanying video game! No need to convert the models or even switch applications.

2. The game engine is fairly robust and really accessible in terms of its difficulty of use. In fact at times animators will find it easier to create a mini-game to act out a scene, and just keep playing it until the scene is played out as desired (as was done to animate a car chase scene). In fact, there are several legitimate non-gaming uses of the game engine that are ably enumerated in the following article:

http://www.blendernation.com/2006/12/03/using-blenders-game-engine-for-more-than-just-games/

3. Blender is itself Open Source and released under the GPL license, and we have already discussed why it is so

awesome.

4. There are multiple repositories of free downloadable models and even animation available (this is a case where the Open Source culture applies to more than just source code). For example, we were able to download a chessboard for this book from the following link (which made the examples much cooler than using the plain cube): http://www.blender-models.com/model-downloads/objects/id/chessboard/

5. In addition to repositories there are several Open Movie Projects where, for the price of a DVD, you can get not only the movie, but the models and blender files used in many of the scenes. This is one of the more compelling aspects, because you can leap frog your own modeling since the models themselves can be reused, modified, and incorporated into your projects.

6. Profitable games have been developed using the game engine such as Color Cube, Dead Cyborg and Nicoles Nel collection.

7. It has been used in the production of major films such as Spider-Man 2, Friday or Another Day, The Secret of Kells, and various History Channel programs.

8. If you are a Lightworks fan, it integrates very well. Also, unlike Lightworks, the documentation knows no bounds, there are a ton of books, e-books, manuals, online tutorials, and demonstration videos to help you do pretty much anything you are trying to accomplish.

9. You have chosen the best time to start using Blender (as opposed to any time prior to the 2.5 release). The latest version about to come out is 2.67 which promises some great bug fixes and incremental improvements to the recently overhauled gaming engine.

10. You can extend its functionality very easily with Python scripting, which this book will demonstrate. Python is a very worthwhile language to pick up as we will get into in the next chapter.

The bottom line is that you have made an excellent decision in choosing to learn and use Blender 3D. Moreover, your interest in extending its capabilities with Python scripting is sure to pay off.

IN OUR NEXT CHAPTER...

Now that we have covered the basics of Blender and her incredible awesomeness, we will move onto the gallant Python and we'll see what Blender sees in him.

Along Came a Python…

CHAPTER TWO – PYTHON CIRCLES BLENDER

While Blender 3D is not completely coded in Python, it is shipped with an embedded Python interpreter that allows you to write Python scripts for Blender. In addition, the Blender Python API (bpython) is available to these scripts, giving the scripts access to the programs inner workings (Objects, Menus, Mesh, UV, etc) which opens up a world of possibilities.

Before getting too deep into the details, lets address why this is so great for you. Blender 3D is open source, which means if you really wanted to, you could make whatever changes you wanted to make to the source code, and recompile the whole suite. You are welcome to do this, and many have, but this is not what this book is about, and in most cases this isn't needed or even preferable.

The problem for most people trying to update Blender's source code is the complexity of Blender itself. Also, not everyone wants to have to familiarize themselves with the vast ocean of source code when they can simply create a script within the program to extend its functionality.

Also, a major drawback of messing with the source code directly is that it makes it difficult for you to take an upgrade and maintain your modifications (putting you in the difficult position of having to choose between a new Blender release and your personal modifications). When python scripts are used, they can often be seamlessly moved to the new version with few if any changes needed (occasionally changes are made to the API or Python version that will require minor adjustments to scripts).

Independent of its connection to Blender, Python is a fantastic language. The Python language itself is Open Source. It is very readable and easy to pick up for anyone familiar with Object Oriented Programming (OOP) basics. Python also leverages several features that shorten the development cycle such as **Duck Typing** mentioned earlier. Duck Typing is basically the idea that if something *walks* like a duck and *looks* like a duck and *quacks* like a duck then for all intents and purposes **it is a duck**. This comes into play with interoperability of objects, functions and methods. In many traditional programming languages, if you want to use a function for an object type it wasn't explicitly defined for, then at a minimum they will need to share a parent object or one will need to inherit from the other. In Duck Typing, the method will try to run with the passed object regardless of inheritance. If the Object passed has the needed properties, operators, and methods expected by the function, then it will work properly during run time. Otherwise, it will error again but at run time, not design time. Critics will complain that this makes testing harder, but for your purposes trust me, this is not a major issue and you will appreciate the forgiving but stable nature of Python.

Another benefit of learning and using Python with Blender is that Python is a fully fledged programming language that can be used to code just about anything, from CGI scripts and development IDE's, to web development and video games. In fact, after learning about Python I found that two games I had played extensively were completely coded up in Python.

Just like with Blender, if you are going to spend your valuable time learning something, it might as well be on a powerful platform that will not limit you down the road. Python is no joke, as you are likely starting to appreciate; it is used by large companies like Google and HP extensively. Often times a task can be accomplished with a fraction of the lines of code needed, since Python always errs on the side of supporting rapid development. Structure rarely gets in the way with Python, and yet it maintains a readability edge over other scripting languages such as Perl script.

The bottom line is that Blender has made an excellent choice in choosing Python as the scripting language to work with its API, and you have made an excellent choice deciding to pick up these two powerful open source offerings.

IN OUR NEXT CHAPTER...

While this volume is not intended to, in any way, be an in-depth work on either Blender or Python, it will show us the basics in terms of getting started and help point us in the right direction to dig deeper. In the next chapter we will ask the simple yet burning question every developer has when they approach a new development environment, namely: Where does the code go?

CHAPTER THREE – WHERE DOES THE CODE GO?

The first question I always have when approaching a new development environment is, "where does the code go?"

After that, I want to know, "how do I run/compile/execute the code and see the results?" And once I have all that, just give me the standard documentation and a week or so, and I should know my way around.

So that's what we are going to do in this chapter, and we can start with addressing where the code goes. First of all, if you have a traditional programing background, keep in mind that you are not really coding and compiling, rather you are scripting and interpreting.

The difference may appear subtle, but the main takeaway is that your Python scripts will be entered right into the Blender Suite (in other words, you won't be using an external IDE to compile your code; instead you can use an editor like Notepad++ like we did for the code examples in this volume, and then cut and paste your script directly into Blender 3D, which has a built-in Python *interpreter* that can run the code and register any operators and such referenced in your script.

Let's take a look at a very simple script just so we can see where the scripts are put and how they are run. For this example, we are going to use the infamous cube that appears when Blender is first started for our model.

First, let's take a look at the first example script:

Figure 1: *Move Square By Two Spaces Script*

```
MoveByTwo.py
1    #To access Blenders components import the "bpy"
2    #or bpython module to give access
3    #to the python interpreter
4    import bpy
5
6    class MoveTwoOperator(bpy.types.Operator):
7        bl_idname = "object.movetwo_operator"
8        bl_label = "Move Two Operator"
9
10       def execute(self, context):
11           context.active_object.location.x += 2.0
12           return {'FINISHED'}
13
14   def register():
15       bpy.utils.register_class(MoveTwoOperator)
16
17   if __name__ == "__main__":
18       register()
```

This is the code we will use to start with. Instead of saying, "Hello World!", we are going to be much more subtle about it and just anti-climatically move the square by two spaces along the X axis.

We will break down this code a bit later, but for now let's see where we put it first. If you open a new Blender project you should notice something similar to the following:

Figure 2: The Not-So-Exciting Blender Starting Point

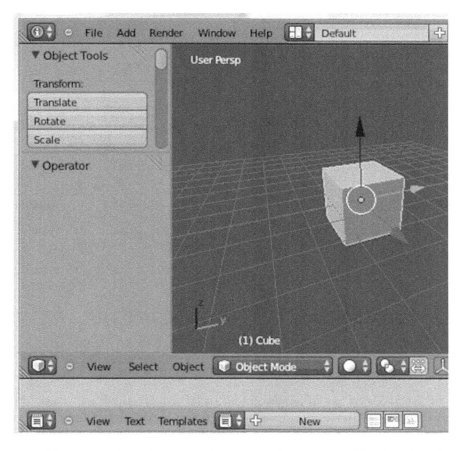

Okay, so depending on how you have your Blender install configured it might look a little different, but you get the idea. Now on the bottom pane, make sure you set the Editor Type to Text Editor so it looks like the figure above.

Then click the white plus sign looking symbol and change the name of the text file (unless you think "text" is sufficiently descriptive); we will call ours "MoveByTwo" and then copy and paste our code from **Figure 1** (as pictured below) and click the "Run Script" button to the right, or press Alt+P if you like to spaz out on shortcuts.

Figure 3: *Starting Block With Python Script in Text Editor*

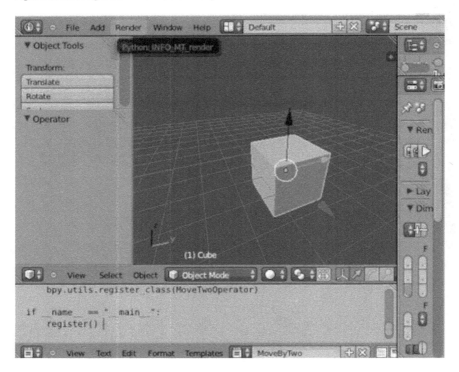

So to answer your question THAT is where the code goes. As satisfying as it was to find that out and run your first python script, it may leave you with the underwhelming feeling that nothing happened from running your script.

In fact, a lot happened in this script but we haven't used the functionality that has been added. To get the satisfaction of seeing your code in action, make sure the cube is selected by right-clicking it. Once selected, simply click on the space bar and start typing "Move Two Operator" and select it once you see it an. This menu is more or less a search screen for operators **including** the operator you just coded and registered.

"Move By Two" Example Breakdown

So now you know where to put your code, let's add a simple operator, and then get access to that operator so you can execute it. But first, let's take a moment to analyze the code we plugged in (we will briefly touch on this, because this volume is not meant to be a lesson on Python or re-iterate what is in the bpython API documentation, but is meant to jumpstart you into using Python with Blender and get you ramped up to the point that you can use the API documentation with minimal confusion).

In line 3 we see "import bpy" and again, this is what brings in the blender specific class for the API. You should know that according to Blender's own documentation, "any setting that can be changed via a button can also be changed from Python". So think of **bpy** as being the programmatic version of the Blender GUI in its entirety. Then, there are multiple subsets of **bpy** to access different aspects of Blender; for example **bpy.data** gives you access to the current blend file which you will use extensively.

Starting with line 6 down to line 12 is where **our operator is defined**. It starts off in line 6 with a Class definition which might confuse the beginner, but just remember that all Operators are Classes but not all Class definitions are of operators per se. In lines 7 and 8 we simply **define some properties that Blender cares about**. This is the sort of thing that is documented in Blenders API which you will need to familiarize yourself with as you get more and more immersed into Python scripting within Blender (and again this book is meant to take care of any prerequisite knowledge you need to understand what to do with the API documentation). In this example, **bl_idname** and **bl_label** are properties that already exist when you define **MoveTwoOperator** because it was defined using **bpy.types.Operator,** which is Blender's standard definition for Operators to be used within the application.

The **bl_idname** is being given the "object" prefix in its value because this is a convention that identifies the operator as related to a Blender object, instead of texture or a mesh. All of the blender specific default properties should have the "bl_" prefix which will make it easy when looking at scripts to separate your custom properties from blenders standard ones. The purpose of this property is to provide an internal identifier for this property, should it be used in other scripts.

The **bl_label** is what is seen in the operator search screen by the end user (as in you from two minutes ago when you were searching for the operator to execute on our exciting cube here).

Lines 9 through 11 are used to define our first function which is going to hold the guts of what our operator actually does when the user chooses it. Notice in line 10 the **active_object** of the context is being used, which is why we had to make sure that the object was selected by right clicking it prior to running our operator. There is a collection (or array) of all the objects and we could have accessed it that way, but of course that is a little more complicated (especially when there are multiple objects in the context).

Every context object (which of course includes the **active_object**) has a location property/object and every location has **x**, **y**, and **z** properties. In this case we are simply increasing the **x** position property by two.

Now if we look to lines 13 and 14 we see a **register** function defined. In this function, we need to call the **register_class** method that is kept in the **utils** class that is part of the **bpy** library. Unlike **bpy.data** which gives you access to the current blend file, **bpy.utils** has a collection of utility type methods and such that help to manipulate the menus, buttons, and other aspects of blender. In lines 16 and 17 we are more or less running the **register** function we just defined.

One thing that perplexed me when approaching Python was that lines of code, and arguably methods and functions, do not have clear demarcations indicating when they end and the next line begins.

Notepad++ will group them, which you can see inbetween the row numbers and the actual code (you can even collapse chunks of code). If they don't look right in Notepad++ then you likely haven't formatted the code correctly.

It is worth noting as well that the **MoveTwoOperator** definition ends at line 11 (and in the Notepad++ screenshot above you can see the grouping ending on line 11). Logically this is needed. The **register** function passes it as an argument to the **register_class** method.

IN OUR NEXT CHAPTER...

Thus far, we have been dealing with the starting cube we have all grown to know and love. But what if that isn't enough for us? What if we wanted something more to sink our teeth into? Should we kill half a tree in this book modeling out something more interesting (even though this book really isn't about modeling)? Is there something better? Is there somewhere we could turn to so we can get a little jumpstart? (Hint: answers coming shortly in the next chapter).

Justin Valencia and Jordan Robert Kaufman

CHAPTER FOUR – AWESOME PUBLIC DOMAIN CHESS SET

Remember when I told you that besides gaining access to an ocean of premium quality free software, that another benefit of engaging in the Open Source community was the community itself? Well, if you already have a background with Blender, then you are likely already familiar with this concept.

I mean besides the Blender suite itself, you have access to freely available scripts, plugins, BVH files (for motion capture), and my personal favorite: plenty of free – in every sense of the word – models, there just for the taking!

Hey, we could spend the rest of this volume manipulating the starting cube (and, that Blender, she knows how much I love playing mind games on hexahedrons) but you and I are too awesome for that (I mean we both did choose to throw down on the side of her majesty, Lady Blender). So instead, we will leverage the work already done and shared by the community at large. If you want to download the chess set we will be using, you can get it from the following location: http://www.blender-models.com/model-downloads/objects/id/chessboard/

Once you have that downloaded and extracted open the "chessboard" blend file. You will notice that the pieces were lovingly provided along with the chessboard. The author makes a comment on an internal note that the pieces need work, especially the knight, but I actually think they look great – especially for our purposes.

When you have it opened up it should look like the following:

Figure 4: *The Awesome Public Domain Chess Set*

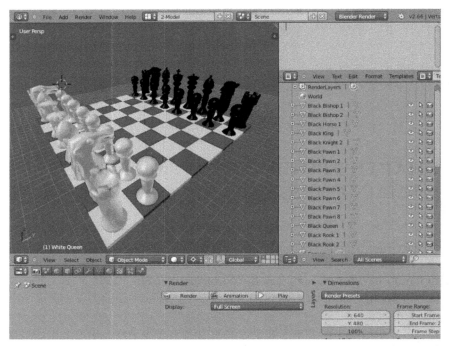

Now that we have this complete chess set at our disposal, we will start using it in conjunction with some examples that are very similar in nature to those in the previous chapter, but with a much more useful/awesome application than nudging hexahedra along the x axis.

First let's start by moving a white pawn as we would in a real game of standard chess (sorry monster chess fans) and for easy visibility I will start with the Clemenz Opening (which I'm sure my Estonian readers will appreciate – *nerd joke I know*) so I will need to move my rightmost white pawn. But first we need to give Python another script so he can help us out here.

Make sure the view on the bottom pane (or whichever) is set to Text Editor, and choose to add a new text block and add the following code:

Figure 5: *Move White Pawn One Square Forward Script*

```
MoveWhitePawn.py
 1    import bpy
 2
 3    class MoveWhitePawn(bpy.types.Operator):
 4        bl_idname = "object.movewhitepawn_operator"
 5        bl_label = "Move White Pawn."
 6
 7        def execute(self, context):
 8            context.active_object.location.y += 2.75
 9            return {'FINISHED'}
10
11    def register():
12        bpy.utils.register_class(MoveWhitePawn)
13
14    if __name__ == "__main__":
15        register()
```

You can tell by examining the above that not much has changed except for some names, which coordinate is being incremented and by how much the object is moving on the axis. Actually sounds like a lot, but besides line 8 only the names/labels have been changed.

Now after we run this script the "**Move White Pawn**" operator will be registered with blender and we can select an object, press space bar, and search for it in the list of other operators.

Keep in mind that while we are using chess piece terms to describe the examples in this chapter, these operators will operate on **any object** that appears in this blend file. In fact, even the chessboard itself can be moved using the "**Move White Pawn**" operator… but that movement would not make any sense for the purposes of chess (hence the naming conventions used in this chapter).

Once you have an active object (in my case the white pawn all the way to right) and you have found and executed the new operator from the list of available operators, your screen should look very much like mine below:

Figure 6: Move White Pawn (Clemenz Opening)

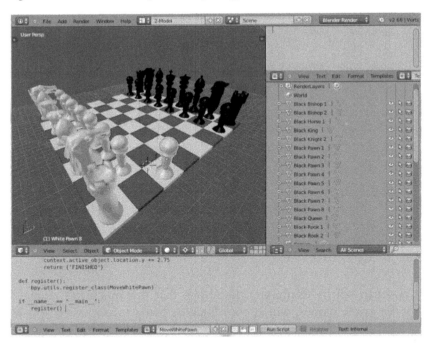

Now the next thing we are going to do is repeat this for Black, but we cannot use the same operator because that would have the pawns moonwalking, which is not a legal chess move. You will notice below that the code for "**Move Black Pawn**" is nearly identical to "**Move White Pawn**" and the only real functional change is in line 8 where we simply swap out the "+=" operator for the "-=" so that our affected object will move the same distance, as before only in the opposite direction along the y axis:

Figure 7: *Move Black Pawn Forward One Square Script*

```
MoveBlackPawn.py
 1   import bpy
 2
 3   class MoveBlackPawn(bpy.types.Operator):
 4       bl_idname = "object.moveblackpawn_operator"
 5       bl_label = "Move Black Pawn"
 6
 7       def execute(self, context):
 8           context.active_object.location.y -= 2.75
 9           return {'FINISHED'}
10
11   def register():
12       bpy.utils.register_class(MoveBlackPawn)
13
14   if __name__ == "__main__":
15       register()
```

So pick a black pawn to counter with (I will pick a symmetrical response) and you should know the drill by now: right click your object (black pawn) by right clicking it, hit space bar to pull up the search screen for operators, type "**Move Black Pawn**", and choose it.

We will do one more similar example, but this time we will be making more than one change to the object. This will come in handy because we will be moving the Knight, which all chess players know needs to move in two directions each move (or at least you need to move along two axes).

Notice in the following both x and y are decremented and incremented respectively, but the script is otherwise very similar to the last example:

Figure 8: *Move White Knight Forward Left*

```
MoveWhiteKnightLeft.py

 1    import bpy
 2
 3    class MoveWhiteKnightLeft(bpy.types.Operator):
 4        bl_idname = "object.movewhiteknightleft_operator"
 5        bl_label = "Move White Knight Left"
 6
 7        def execute(self, context):
 8            context.active_object.location.y += 5.50
 9            context.active_object.location.x -= 2.75
10            return {'FINISHED'}
11
12    def register():
13        bpy.utils.register_class(MoveWhiteKnightLeft)
14
15    if __name__ == "__main__":
16        register()
```

Again, once you have this in your text editor you can run the script by pressing Alt+P (or press "Run Script"), right click on the white knight you want to use to select it, hit space, and find the new operator you just created, namely "**Move White Knight Left**".

Once you've executed this operator, your board should look something like the following:

Figure 9: *Our Chess Set After Three Turns*

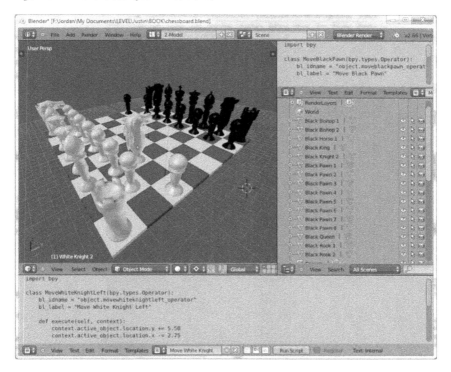

After three turns and three python scripts we should be comfortable with adding operators, registering them, and messing with the active object's location coordinates. In addition, we are comfortable with getting our scripts run within Blender using the embedded Text Editor, and with searching for and executing our operators once they are registered.

IN OUR NEXT CHAPTER...

Now, this has been great in terms of seeing how scripts get run within Blender, but having to search for operators is kind of a drag. In our next chapter we are going to see how to find out what the menus are called internally (within Blender's API), and how to add an operator to an existing menu.

CHAPTER FIVE – ADDING AN OPERATOR TO A MENU

As mentioned earlier, in this chapter we are going to get into how to add one of our snazzy operators to an existing menu. This will make it so we don't have to go searching in the long list of operators every time we want to use it.

However, in order to do that we will need to find out what the name of the menu is internally, so that we will know how it is referenced in the Blender API (and in the bpy module). We are going to add our next operator to the Object menu within the 3D view, so in order to find out what Blender calls that internally, simply hover over the Object menu to get its name like in the following screenshot:

Figure 10: *Hover to Get the Internal Menu Name*

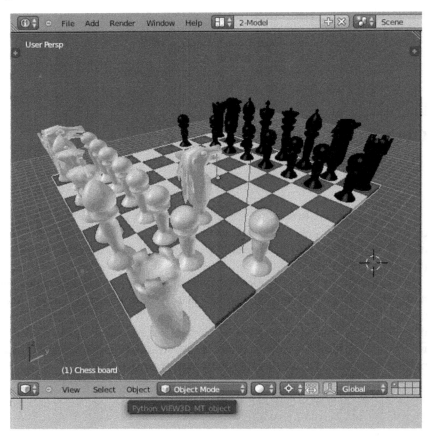

It comes across very muted in print, but you should be able to get the idea that when you hover over pretty much anything in Blender, she will tell you what it is called when trying to access through Python. In this case we can see that the Object menu is known as **VIEW3D_MT_object** internally; we will break down some of the significance of the naming convention later.

For now, we at least have the unique name of the Object menu and we can use this in our next Python script. Once you see how we use it in our Python script, you can swap out any menu name you like and gain access to that menu to add operators, etc.

Notice that in addition to the Menus providing their names upon hovering, even the operators in the menus do so as well.

Be sure to notice how your custom operator is known by Python, by hovering over it once we have it loaded (although don't expect any huge surprises).

In the example coming up, we are going to mimic the initial two-square advance option available to pawns the first time you move a particular pawn for the current game. Then we are going to add this operator to the Objects menu present in the 3D View (as pictured in **Figure 10**).

It may not be immediately apparent to you when you examine the following script, but take a second to notice where we reference the Object menu using the internal name. That's right, we don't need to reference it until we are ready to register our operator with the menu, which means that nothing about our operator definition itself needs to change to make it menu register-able – so to speak:

Figure 11: Adding an Operator to a Menu

```
MoveWhitePawnOpenerWITHBUTTON.py
1    #This moves the white pawn forward two spaces
2    #and puts a button for this on the Object menu
3    import bpy
4
5    class WhitePawnOpener(bpy.types.Operator):
6        """White Pawn Opener"""   #Blender uses this as tool-tip
7        bl_idname = "object.whitepawnopener_operator"
8        bl_label = "White Pawn Opener"
9
10       def execute(self, context):
11           context.active_object.location.y += 5.50
12           return {'FINISHED'}
13
14   def add_object_button(self, context):
15       self.layout.operator(
16           WhitePawnOpener.bl_idname,
17           text=WhitePawnOpener.__doc__,
18           icon='PLUGIN')
19
20   def register():
21       bpy.utils.register_class(WhitePawnOpener)
22       bpy.types.VIEW3D_MT_object.append(add_object_button)
23
24   if __name__ == "__main__":
25       register()
```

If you don't get any error after executing this script in the Text Editor, then our new "**White Pawn Opener**" not only will have our new operator registered into the pool of available operators, but we will have registered it with the Object menu (**VIEW3D_MT_object**). The new operator should appear at the top of the menu, so you may need to scroll to the top (as I needed to, since I have a scrunched screen size that I am using so the screen shot size works with this book's trim size).

"White Pawn Opener" Example Breakdown

We have already discussed the extra register line that we see in **Figure 11** on line 22, but what has been registered there? We see that **add_object_button** is the argument passed to the append method for the menu we are working with.

While our class definition for **WhitePawnOpener** (lines 5 – 12 above) is strikingly similar to the previous examples, we see another definition prior to the registry, namely **add_object_button** starting at line 14.

In this definition, **add_object_button** is passed two arguments, namely **self** and **context**. We've already discussed **context** earlier, but in this case **self** is being used to access it's **layout.operator()** function where the layout is the current menu (so later when we register is when it actually knows which menu to add this too – so in a way **self** is serving as a placeholder).

Then within **add_object_button** we pass three arguments to the **operator()** function. The first is to give it the internal name of the operator in question; the second is for what will be used as a label/tooltip; the last argument is simply to identify which icon to use next to our operator when it appears in the menu (in our example we used the stock 'PLUGIN' icon, which you will see once you've executed this script and go looking for your operator in the Objects menu).

You can see all of this in the following screenshot:

Figure 12: Our Operator Appears in the Object Menu

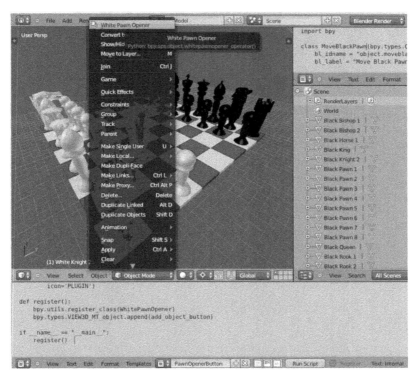

So now we see a few important things: our "White Pawn Operator" has been added to the Object menu, we can see the standard icon calling out this operator as a plugin, so now we can execute our operator on a selected object without having to search for the operator by name (instead we can simply find the operator in the Objects menu).

Please note that although this operator has been added to the menu, it is only permanent for *this blender session* and if you close blender and open a new file, it will not appear in the menu. For that, the menu will need to be installed.

I hope by this point you are starting to get a sense of the extent to which Blender can be customized.

With hover tooltips that give you the internal name of each menu and operator, an embedded text editor that can run (or rather interpret) Python scripts, a Python console (that we haven't even messed with yet), and a very well documented and exhaustive API, it is like the Blender Foundation is just asking you to crack this thing open and start making improvements (actually I think they actually do come just short of begging the developer community to do so, and have certainly made it easy for us).

IN OUR NEXT CHAPTER...

So now we know what Blender and Python are (Chapters One and Two), we know where the code goes (Chapter Three), we laid down some operator kung fu on our awesome public domain chess set (Chapter Four), and we have even added our home made operator to a menu in this chapter.

So what next? Well, remember when we said that our operator would only be on the Objects menu for the current session? This means that we would need to run our last script again when we started a new session (ie. came back the next day) and that would turn out to be pretty lame after a while. So, in our next chapter we will learn how we can actually install our add on so that it will stay on the menu until we want to get rid of it. I mean, now that Blender and Python have been thoroughly introduced, it is about time for something a little more longer term than a cheap one-*session*-stand (please email me with any complaints about the nerd comedy and maybe I'll tone it down in the next volume, well... maybe).

CHAPTER SIX – INSTALLING YOUR MIGHTY ADDON

So by now, you are feeling the power of Python and his ability to extend Blender without too much trouble. If you don't fully appreciate it at this point however, maybe we should review a few things.

First, we could be dealing with a closed source proprietary 3D system that essentially cannot be extended by the users (and believe me there are a plethora of those types of suites out there). In this case we could submit an enhancement request through some support link and wait patiently as our newborn children grow up and start attending grade school, and by the time they have their long division down, voila! We have our new feature at our finger tips. Not too exciting but if you have a decade or so to spare, then this approach works great.

Secondly, even if we were using another open source application that we wanted to extend, it isn't necessarily that much easier for the casual (or even average) coder to make adjustments, because access to source code is just the first step. On some open source projects, you either need to be an expert on the language being used, or you at least have to get very familiar with the inner workings of the open source offering you are working on. Still, this is much better than dealing with a proprietary system when, unless you have stacks (and I mean STACKS) of cash or you are dreaming, you will never see the source code. Remember, my boss at Level was part of a closed-source proprietary code transfer at one time that had to involve over a million dollars, armed guards, and a handcuffed brief case being personally delivered by their partner software vendor.

Lastly, as if open source wasn't enough, Blender provides this lightweight but powerful Python Interpreter to process python scripts that can be coded without having to recompile the entire Blender suite, or having to have too much intimate knowledge on the inner workings of Blender's source code (that probably isn't exhaustively documented anyhow).

Instead, we have access to all the pertinent parts of Blender (both of the current blend and the Blender menus, etc) with a well-documented API that can be found at the following link:

http://www.blender.org/documentation/blender_python_api_2_6 7_release/

The API will prove extremely helpful as you get deeper into extending Blender's functionality. Again, this small volume wasn't meant to be a lesson on Blender 2.6 (or even Python 3), but rather it was meant simply to show you where to get started, and to make sure that step by step directions were given, and the examples would be broken down. When we got started, there was already a ton of information online (thank you oh-wondrous interweb!) but the examples were rarely broken down. Also, sometimes you just need a book, in my opinion, and there wasn't a real good volume that addressed extending blender with Python at the beginner level (or at least not any for Blender 2.6x). Plus, we intend for this to be the first in a series, but wanted to get something out quickly with a low price point to see if there is the need we think there is for this type of targeted volume. We'll get into our future plans a little later.

Back to the lesson at hand. If we are going to be spending any considerable amount of time scripting, then we are going to want to develop code that we can code once and reap the benefits of for months and even years to come. And we don't want to have to run our scripts again every time we fire up Blender, now do we?

No we do not. So we will need to install our mighty add-on so that it will be part of our blender experience until we choose to toggle it off under User Preferences (more on that later).

The following script accomplishes the same basic function as our previous script only is prepared to be installed as an add-on (as our code gets longer it gets harder to keep the same text size so even if you can't read it just download the code examples if you haven't already from: https://snipt.net/BlenderMeetsPython/).

Figure 13: Our Operator Ready for Install

```
     MoveWhitePawnOpenerWITHAddOn.py
 1     #Same as last Script but prepared to be installed add-on
 2     bl_info = {
 3         "name": "White Opener",
 4         "category": "Object",
 5     }
 6
 7     import bpy
 8
 9     class WhitePawnOpener(bpy.types.Operator):
10         """White Pawn Opener"""    #Blender uses this as tool-tip
11         bl_idname = "object.whitepawnopener_operator"
12         bl_label = "White Pawn Opener"
13         bl_options = {'REGISTER', 'UNDO'}
14
15         def execute(self, context):
16             context.active_object.location.y += 5.50
17             return {'FINISHED'}
18
19     def add_object_button(self, context):
20         self.layout.operator(
21             WhitePawnOpener.bl_idname,
22             text=WhitePawnOpener.__doc__,
23             icon='PLUGIN')
24
25     def register():
26         bpy.utils.register_class(WhitePawnOpener)
27         bpy.types.VIEW3D_MT_object.append(add_object_button)
28
29     def unregister():
30         bpy.utils.unregister_class(WhitePawnOpener)
31
32     if __name__ == "__main__":
33         register()
```

The **bl_info** being defined in lines 2 to 5 is going to be used by the User Preferences view within Blender. This is where all the add-ons appear and can be toggled on and off after install.

Besides that, the changes are somewhat minimal. Line 13 just opens up the option for this add-on to be toggled on and off (registered/deregister) with the help of lines 29 and 30 where, for the first time, we have defined an **unregister** method. This will be used to toggle off the add on should it not suit the current work you are doing.

When we go to install this code, you will notice (possibly unbeknownst to you previously) that your add-on is not alone and that Blender ships with quite a few out-of-the-box add-ons. Part of the reason these add-ons weren't incorporated into the actual source code for blender (and instead left as add-ons) is that they may have originated from users just like you that created an Add-On using Python to provide some small block of unavailable functionality, and then shared their work (which you are more than encouraged to do yourself – in fact please email me any Python scripts you code and want to share after reading this volume, I would love to see it: iwmsconsultant@gmail.com).

Okay, so did I mention that we are not going to be running this script in the usual way? No, in fact we are going to install it, so here are the steps to do just that:

1. Make sure you have your **script saved as a file** (and keep to the Python conventions, most importantly save it with a ".py" extension). I have found if I try and place the script in the directory that Blender uses, Blender doesn't like this – it wants to put the Add-On scripts there, so watch for that and just save your file initially

2. Then in the info pane (which I usually keep up top, as it's by default) click **File –> User Preferences** (alternately you could have pressed ctrl-alt-U and been cool like me).

3. From the User Preferences screen click the "**Install from File...**" button (please note that we are using Blender 2.66 for all of these examples but your button may say something slightly different if you have yet to upgrade).

4. Locate your "*.py" file (NOTE: remember we said the "py" extension was important?) and click "Install from File..." but this time you will see that button at the top right (as shown Figure 14 below).

5. Now technically the add-on has been installed at this point but you may not see it take effect. *The reason being is that while Blender allows you to extend its application with the use of add-on's it always allows the user to toggle on and off any as-shipped or custom/user installed add-ons.* To toggle on your newly installed add-on click "File" -> User Preferences (or simply type Ctrl+Alt+U) and in the screen that appears, make sure the "Addons" group is selected and click the Disabled category in the left section of the User Preference Screen (See Figure 15 below).

6. Then click on the checkbox and you will see that your add-on appears to disappear. Don't worry, this is simply because your add-on is no longer *disabled* so it no longer appears in the disabled category. If, for whatever reason there are many disabled add-ons to start with, you can simply type "White Opener" in the search box in the upper left (again pictured in

Figure 15).

7. At this point, your add-on should be installed and enabled. To confirm that everything was done correctly, make sure that the "White Pawn Operator" appears in the Object menu.

Figure 14: *Picking Your Python File for Installation*

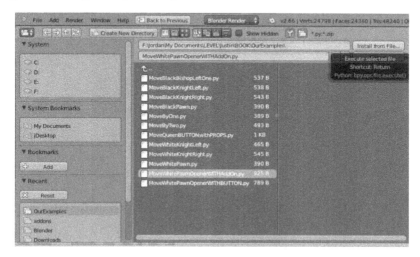

Now keep in mind that this is just one way to install an add-on, but this is the most likely approach you will use for any of your own scripts; however, if you were trying to package your extensions into an installer for other users to make use of, (possibly after paying for such an add-on) then there are other installation methods out there.

Do not worry if you see multiple entries of the "White Pawn Operator" in the Object menu since we have been going through multiple examples.

Next time you start Blender you should just see the entry from the installed/enabled example.

Figure 15: *Enabling Your Installed Add-On*

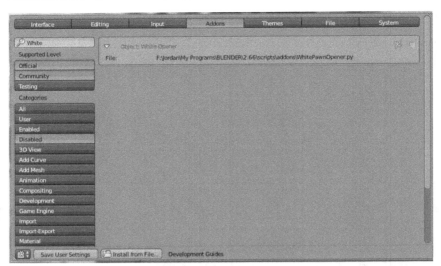

"Install Add-On" Example Breakdown

We don't really need to breakdown the code too much, since this is very similar to the previous example. In addition we have already discussed **bl_info** and the new **unregister** method which are the major code changes from the previous example's code.

That said, you can see that the defined "name" and "category" information within **bl_info** gets used in the User Preferences screen. You may have noticed that not all the add-ons are in the same category: some are "3D View", some are for the "Import-Export" category, but of course we find ours under "Object" since we designated that in the **bl_info** clause we added. Also we see that the User Preference screen used our add-on name of "White Opener" that we find in line 3 in Figure 13 above.

Besides that, you don't really see the **unregister** directly, but you see its effect whenever you disable your add-on.

IN OUR NEXT CHAPTER...

So we now know the basics in terms of where our Python Scripts need to go, how to manipulate our context or current Blend file, and how to temporarily or permanently make additions to the menus within the Blender application itself.

What, though, do we actually do with this information? When should we crack out our scripting skills and when do we find another solution? Where do we go from here and what reference material will be indispensable to us? All this and more in our next chapter.

Justin Valencia and Jordan Robert Kaufman

CHAPTER SEVEN – NEXT STEPS

Getting right into it: **when should we crack out our scripting skills,** and when do we find another solution? Well, I would generally consider creating my own Python script as a last resort (*technically second to last resort because last resort would be actually changing Blender's source code and recompiling but "homie don't play that" if you know what I mean*). So what would be preferable to writing your own Python script (despite the inherent joy that brings)? Below is a sort of hierarchy of script sources I've put together (just start at the top and work your way down until you find a solution):

1. **Enabled and Included Add-Ons.** The add-ons that are most likely to be used most by the most people are the ones that already ship with Blender (to a very large extent, the Blender Foundation development team – as small as it is – are really on top of the needs of the community). Among the add-ons shipped with Blender, many of them are toggled *off* by default. Obviously they are assuming that you are more likely to use the Enabled (or toggled *on*) add-ons, so you might want to review these to see if you are missing functionality staring you right in the face. The cool thing about this is that when we are in User Preferences -> Addons section -> and choose the Enabled category, we can drill into the add-on that interests us, and in most cases there is a "Link to the Wiki" button that will take us right to a page that will give us more detail on the add-on in question (our example didn't provide the info for that so check another add-on, like "Import-Export: STL format" for example).

2. **Disabled but Included Add-Ons.** Next inline are the

add-ons that are shipped with Blender, but are disabled (toggled *off*) by default. The fact that they are not Enabled by default does not make them any less important, again the Blender Foundation is really looking out for "what will most people need when they get started", and not for what will be your personal optimal setup. Of course, you can see these by switching to the Disabled category in the User Preferences editor in the Addons section.

3. **Already-Existing Scripts Online.** If none of the As-Shipped options suit what you are looking for, then try finding Scripts online published by some other proud open-source developer. One such collection can be found at the following link, but keep in mind that this has already aged and many of the scripts will by now have either been incorporated into Blender 2.66 or will no longer work with the current version (although the harm for the later is limited – out of date scripts typically just cease to function and rarely cause fatal issues within Blender): http://www.blendernation.com/2009/07/14/blender-python-scripts-catalog/

4. **Scripts In Development.** Remember that awesome open source Blender community we raved about earlier? Well one way of getting what you need is to ask the community. Now, since scripts aren't nearly as complicated as developing the Blender suite itself (that the circuits it is not) don't expect to have a formal collaborative project to help out with in terms of putting scripts together. That said, the community is very helpful especially when you clearly explain what you are trying to do, and it helps to provide the code from your first attempt. The following is a great example where one user posts his question, along with his blend file which has his logic bricks that he wants converted into Python scripts, and another user gives him the scripts he needs (and we can all enjoy): http://blenderartists.org/forum/showthread.php?260783-Movement-Script-Need-help-changing-logic-bricks-to-python-script

5. **Lay Down The Py-Fu!** Ultimately, if you are so unsatisfied with Blenders base functionality, you get no satisfaction from the shipped enabled and disabled add-ons, and there are no Python scripts online that suit you it

may be time to lay down the Python-Fu and get coding. (By the way, in the previous bullet I wasn't suggesting that you should try and push off your scripting work to the community and free-ride, what I *was* trying to say is that you can ask the community if they've solved similar problems with Python scripting (and if so sharing can commence) and also, if you are stuck you can ask for help; when it comes to Open Source software it really helps if everyone tries to be a giver and not all takers (*like everything in life really*). When you are done think whether your code would be useful to others, and if so pop onto your favorite Blender blog and post it (email me the link to – I would just love that)!

Remember though that most of the times when we wish that Blender did something that it doesn't appear to do, that it actually does do it (in other words this is a knowledge gap in us rather than a functionality gap in the product). Of course, remember that there are many ways to skin a creeper and that it's okay to code something up that you might have been able to accomplish some other way. Often a simple script that does exactly what we want will be more efficient than some tool that abstracts our workflow (as was the case in the Blender Artists example above where he want's logic bricks converted to Python scripts).

The Robust Blender API… Documentation

So, where do we go from here, and what reference material will be indispensable to us? Well that all depends on our background. If we came to this book with Python expertise, but no idea how to use it within the framework, then the most important resource is going to be Blenders API. For that you can go directly to the following: http://www.blender.org/documentation/blender_python_api_2_67_1/

Now we obviously didn't think this browser based wiki-style documentation was the easiest for new-comers, or we wouldn't have put together this basic volume to smooth the transition; and this really isn't a crack at the Blender Foundations documentation at all – in fact many find it a great way to get started. Everyone thinks a little differently and for my taste, I don't like approaching any kind of wiki until I already know what I am looking for from the site. Put another way, have you ever gone to Wikipedia simply to browse or to systematically acquire a well-rounded education in a short focused period of time? Not likely! Instead you search it out when you have something already in mind that you are looking for, and then maybe you get lost in its interconnected linked web of useful write-ups until it occurs to you that 20 minutes ago you got the info you needed, you don't really need the entire history of how the MIT License was developed and you really should get back to writing your book, so that by the time it is published Blender 3.0 isn't already being released! Okay, maybe that last part was more me-centric but you get my point.

I will say, however, that while the Blender API Documentation feels distinctively like every other wiki you have ever used, it does start and end with two useful features that help reduce the wiki-wasteland effect a bit.

First they start with a "Blender/Python Documentation" section with some general articles to get yourself comfortable with scripting with Python. Between their Quickstart, API Overview, and their Addon Tutorial, you really should have what you need to get started. We of course felt that the tutorial, especially, brings the user along very quickly, which is to be expected in any wiki-documentation setting (again, hence the book you are holding in your hands).

The second thing I find really useful is that after all the Modules are listed (they are broken up into Application, Standalone and Game Engine) there is a section called "API Info" where they keep track of the changes to the API between versions. I think in general I would prefer if they started with the most recent API changes, but either way this will help you keep your head straight, especially if you are sticking with a version until you finish an in-depth scripting project, and then switch to porting to the most recent version (which is usually a fair approach). In that case, you can simply start at the version you developed in, and walk through the changes to the API. If you are the solo developer on your project, you should recognize classes that you work with as you review each change, and then can make the needed changes. With multiple developers you can either make each developer go through the same process, or use a consolidated change log (if Code Reviews some other SDLC process is being followed to compile changes) to walk through the release notes.

Getting back to the Modules listed in the first page of the API Documentation, a quick glance will show that we've already touched on a few of these modules such as **bpy.context, bpy.data, bpy.types**, and **bpy.ops**. Now it should be obvious by now that we only scratched the surface of these modules, but the tools are now at your fingertips to dig deeper into them. Plus, even the small handful of exercises we have had you walk through have put these modules into context, and you will be surprised how helpful that will be when digging into the API Documentation further. Of course we are planning future volumes that get much deeper into useful applications of Python Scripting within Blender, but we don't expect (or even want) you to wait for those.

Still Scared of Python?

Would it help if I told you that the Python is more scared of *you* than you are of *it*? I guess not. Well if you are still wishing that you had more basic or advanced knowledge of Python, there are options.

If you want to quickly get up on the very basics of Python and get coding quickly (outside of Blender at least for the exercises), and feel like you know the basic keywords and syntax and such, then I highly recommend "**Python In A Day**" by Richard Wagstaff. Be warned though that he is not exaggerating when he says that you can get everything out of this book in a single day. If you have Amazon Prime, then you can check it out for free which is great (if not you have to decide if it is worth it – I will say it gets you coding quickly).

If you are looking for more a Blender-specific Python scripting book, unfortunately I can only really recommend "**Blender 2.49 Scripting**" by Michel Anders. Now, Anders is a great technical writer, but it does hurt to blow most of two twenties on a book that uses a pre-Blender 2.6 version. I really hope he puts out a new addition, (on the other hand I may never have written this volume if he had already – at time of publication there was simply nothing that took on Blender 2.6 scripting directly).

Tony Mullen is a great author that has put out several well received volumes. The one that is most current from him, namely "**Mastering Blender**" does get into Python scripting and the book is not too old (was published on November 28, 2012 according to Amazon).

Now if you are more specifically interested in using Python in conjunction with the Blender Game Engine (BGE,) I don't have a recommendation, per se, but I have pre-ordered (and am eagerly awaiting the release of) a new work called "**Game Development with Blender**" by Mike Pan and Dalai Felinto. The cool thing about this book is that it is at least partially written by the same folks working on the recent updates and fixes to the BGE itself, so maybe they know a thing or two about what they are talking about!

Um, Did I Say I Already Knew Blender?

While we sort of assumed the reader had some basic proficiency in Blender prior to looking into extending it with Python, that assumption is not necessarily correct (nor was such proficiency needed – you basically just needed to already have Blender installed).

However, if you did come about this book completely fresh, or with only previous Python knowledge, then it is my pleasure to highly recommend "**Blender Foundations**" by Roland Hess. Besides being very well written and understandable, it is current (written for 2.6x). Even better than that, Hess approaches the subject with an integrated approach. Let's face it, we are not dealing with a normal business application here. We are not only concerned with learning features of a program, rather we are much more concerned with getting to express the designs and even art that is up until now, stuck in our heads. He discusses standard artistic concepts like representation long before he actually shows you how to do anything. Some find this tedious, but as someone who came at this from a programming (rather than graphical design) background, these insights were greatly appreciated. Trust me, you don't get short changed in terms of technical know-how and you can tell he is a Blender loyalist (it might not mean anything to you but when he gets to the chapter entitled "Sculpting" he actually walks you through this approach in Blender and does skip to some additional external tool you have to learn – he does the sculpting right in Blender).

IN OUR NEXT CHAPTER...

I will reserve comment on any other volumes, since these are the ones I've got my fingers into personally. So in this chapter, we have covered when we will actually be cracking out our own Py-Fu to extend Blender, we have covered where to turn for more information on the Blender API, Python in general, the BGE, and now on expanding our Blender knowledge if needed (**hint**: it's always needed). We are moving right along, although I will point out one topic that I wish a book existed for : how to accomplish professional animation using Machinima concepts, fully expressive face and gesture controls, and doing all of this within Blender using the BGE (plus doing it with an abbreviated workflow since that is the whole point of Machinima anyhow). This is what we plan to address in Volume 2, but we can't leave this exciting niche subject on that note alone.

In our next chapter, we will give you what we consider to be our Mission Statement or Call to Arms (more like Call to Code, but you wouldn't have known what I meant unless I said "Call to Arms" first, now would you?)

There we will discuss a little about the firm I am at, why I wrote this book, and lay out our mission to not only expand Blender's tool set but to be the first to really master the art of Machinima, or Digital Puppetry, and be the ones to take it out the realm of novelty and fanboy diversions and into a legitimate art form (and, hey, revolutionize the world of animation while we're at it, by radically reducing the production time of modern animation). Obviously we are going to need some help along the way to say the least! Some professional background is referenced, so for clarity the next chapter is written exclusively by Jordan Kaufman.

Justin Valencia and Jordan Robert Kaufman

CHAPTER EIGHT – I HAVE BEEN TO THE MODEL TOP

I don't want to give the wrong impression that we are going to somehow change life as we know it on this planet Earth. Nothing so grand I assure you. Technology leaders in the past have sometimes put their work in the place of religion and spirituality, misguidedly implying that their technology is a path to peace with God (as you might conclude after hearing the late Steve Jobs speak). That said, industries have been turned upside down in the past by small handfuls of people who championed an idea whose time had come, and that is exactly what we intend to do.

We may, as isolated individuals, feel that all the great conquest has already been had. Alexander the Great had a similar feeling when his father, Philip II of Macedon, would come home from his conquests when he was just a child. Of course, people don't call his father Philip the Great. The reason we may feel that way ourselves, is that most people focus on areas that already have mature innovations, (desktop computing, mobile phones, etc) and don't look to the spaces that have been missed or long overlooked.

When it comes to animation we have, on the surface at least, what appears to be a very mature and crowded marketplace of technology and talent. While this is mostly true, it ignores a few vitally important components that we need to keep in mind.

First, standard animation as we have come to know it has indeed benefited by many important incremental improvements in workflow, but essentially hasn't changed since the days of the black and white Mickey Mouse cartoons. You are already likely familiar with key-framing, and know that even when each and every frame needed to be hand drawn, that key frames were still used first to block the scenes that needed to be fleshed out later. In a sense the art form took place during this process and then the hordes of outliners, junior animators, and colorists, who would use great technical ability (and you could say *artistic* design), had to be used to layout and accomplish each frame. However, the truth remains that the actual expression (which **decision** is a vital component of) was done during the key framing process.

This remains the same today, only, instead of hordes of junior animators filling in each frame, the frames between the "key" frames are generally computer generated. Now, this is probably the biggest reduction in the production cycle this industry has seen since the concept was hatched in 1650 with the Magic Lantern (which if you think about it, is simply another frame by frame illustration with a low FPS count). So over 350 years of innovation and, while technology has increased and cost has dwindled, the art form still lies in the development of key frames.

Now I know you are thinking to yourself: what about motion capture (MoCap) where you can have a real life ninja in an expensive suite jump around and we can use the data captured in the BVH file and make our models come to life? Or, what about that really cool effect they used in "Waking Life" and "A Scanner Darkly" where they take live action footage as the source of their "animation"? Well, this brings us to our second, and perhaps much more subtle point. In both cases there is in essence **no animator**. In motion capture the model is going through their normal movements and it is being captured (you could hardly say that they are the animator). Then you have a 3D Modeler rig up his model and feed in the MoCap data (either in real time or after the fact) and the model is then *animated* by the fed data. Now I don't want to get into a whole sermon on "What is Art?" or "What Qualifies as Artistic Expression?" but I'm just pointing out that while MoCap is very cool it sort of takes out the animator.

The Art of Projected Animation

So of course MoCap has its place, but it leaves something to be desired for someone that wants to see their vision come to life from mind to art work before they "let go". Also it is largely expensive (especially if you want to do it correctly – please don't email me about Xbox Kinect, I beg you!) so we don't see an explosion of the grassroots animators that I can imagine if we can transcend the chasm that lies between the cartoon visionary and a finished product.

The same applies to the "Scanner Darkly" effect: not only is it costly (again to do correctly) but the actor is providing all the actual *animating* if any is being done by the actor (but it is a great leap to call them animators since they are doing exactly what they would be doing if the film was purely live action).

Perhaps this is a strange definition to you, but I consider someone an animator if they are bringing expressive movement to something outside themselves for the purpose of producing Art. They are providing it, the actual movement, in an expressive form (not by going about their normal bodily movements as in the case of MoCap and "Scanner Darkly"). I guess by this broad definition, a Puppeteer could be called an animator (and I think that is fair). Remember that when we are saying *animation,* we are using the shortened form of what we really mean which is **projected animation** (just like our magic lantern example from history).

See, we are naturally animated, it's even part of our language that we had an "animated" discussion. Meaning we weren't just speaking words but we were *bringing life* to what could have been a lifeless discussion. But a discussion is not a projection and it is not art (however much it may be animated). Our language is us, it is part of who we are, and is not a projection (in fact there is *no credible evidence that mankind has ever lived without a language,* in spite of widespread acceptance that we all had imbecilic grunting ancestors that slowly developed language – where as any study of ancient linguistics bears out the truth that *language appears suddenly and in a highly complex form* that over time became simplified, giving it the advantage of being easy to spread over large distances, so the reverse of what is commonly believed is really the truth, but I digress).

So for my vision of an animator the following is true:
1. The artist **has a vision** of the cartoon or animation they want to bring to life.
2. The artist **has the tools and talent to create** the world and characters and colors that have heretofore been trapped in his mind.
3. The artist **brings these characters and objects to life** (read: motion) directly from nothing else than commands from their mind (we accept no mimicry here – only from mind to controlled medium).

The last component may make your head hurt a little. But we simply cannot accept a computer analyzing someone moving and copying it to be art, or at least not the type of art you call Projected Animation (unless perhaps you are willing to call a robot an artist but I say never!) There must be something else. Clearly put to be a piece of projected animated art (PAA) the artist cannot "let go" until the vision they had trapped in their head has produced the piece of Art (or at least made all the vital decisions that will make it up).

While an animated feature will go through many processes (story boarding, modeling, texturing, editing, color correction, etc.) the piece of it that is the actual animated art, meaning deciding what will move and how each object will be animated must come from the mind of the Animator and stay in his hands, until at least the animation part is complete. This was the case in the old style cartoons, the Animator would work until what was in their minds was down in color, form and at least key frames, which determined both the models and how they would move. The junior "animators" that would come in and complete the in-between frames were just the tool of the true animator as our computers are today.

This is not to say that "Waking Life" is not a piece of art. But it is to say that *that* form of art is called Film (or perhaps Writing, Graphic Design, Acting, etc.) but it is simply not Projected Animated Art (PAA). Projected Animation needs to come from an animator, plain and simple.

So, how will we, after almost 100 years since the establishment of the modern key frame method of projected animation, create the first new addition to the PAA form that is still considered art, still animated and still a projection? Of course all three are needed since dance is an art form that is both *art* and *animated* but it is not *projected* in any way. Furthermore, how will we be able to keep the entire cycle in the hands of a single animator until the animation is complete (all the choices of movement)? Lastly, in so doing will we discover an art form that is both more affordable (read: accessible) and more immediately expressive than any form of animation that preceded it? I believe we will, but where do we start?

Enter Stage Wrong: Machinima

When I mention "Machinima", people either tend to stare at me in confusion over a term that is seldom used outside the circles of fanboy gamers, or they ask me how I am going to create content (for profit)

66

from recording game play and throwing some dumb dialog together, all the while swimming in legally murky water at best.

Well in fact, many of the legal issues have cleared up as game producers have started to release explicit rules for Machinists to abide by and (most likely) not get sued. However the point still stands that this does not seem like a worthwhile venture (despite the fact that the company "Machinima" is raising millions and is one of the top most viewed channels on YouTube).

Really, I could not care less about these legal issues because I am not talking about this type of Machinima. Fanboy Machinima exploits the graphics, animation and controls of already published video games to express themselves in a limited fashion with their main contribution being in voice, over dialog (in the cases where they aren't just dancing around with a bunch of other online unemployables – no offense to the fanboys out there). This can be fun for teenagers to make or watch after a late night of gaming and red bull (when you are so cracked out from the waves of caffeine and sugar highs hitting you in unison circa 2:35 AM) but Pixar has nothing to worry about, I assure you.

Enter Stage Right: Machinima (Digital Puppetry)

What we are championing is what some are terming Digital Puppetry. I'm not in love with that term since it is so broad, but it will do until we can take back the real term which has the perfect meaning for what I am proposing: Machinima, the merging of the machine that is a gaming engine with cinematic expressive animation. And not just a shortcut to avoiding having to actually animate something, but perhaps giving birth to the first pure form of PAA. Let me explain.

Getting right to it, we are proposing taking advantage of the great advancements in gaming technology, specifically in the development of easy-to-use (but powerful) game engines that are now freely available, for the purposes of producing high quality (but low cost), animation.

This is different than just taking advantage already built games, because in that realm you are giving up range of movement, control mechanisms, and in most cases the creation of models and the associated artwork to the hands of the game developers. This is fine for merely "expressing yourself" but it is just giving up too much to still call the work PAA, or more importantly, to be used for serious commercial purposes (even with putting legality aside). What we will do is take the game engine in Blender (which has been derided for not being a serious engine to produce marketable and competitive video games commercially) and use it to create "games" that we can control for the purposes of creating animation. This is Machinima in the fullest sense of the word. In this case the animator will have control both on the "Mach" or machine side (in working with the game engine) and on the more expressive "cinema" side of things, whereas currently machinists are confined to express themselves after the games are created.

This is an important distinction, because the bulk of Machinima has taken place in environments where user-created animation was the last thing on the developers minds (Quake, World of Warcraft, Halo, etc), and even where it is thought about (Second Life, MovieStorm, etc), the emphasis seems to be in creating as realistic objects, people, and settings as quickly as possible. The latter part is great (we all want to reduce workflow time as much as possible), but the fact that all the emphasis is toward creating realistic rather than representative form is unfortunate. You are never going to compete with real live action film, and when you try, you end up looking like you are playing a video game.

Think of it this way: as cool as MovieStorm and especially iClone is when you take a look at what it can do with minimal effort, think to yourself "Self, is anyone going to pay me to create this type of animation?"

The answer is more or less going to be: no. If you think about any work of animation that is close to your heart, so to speak, and compare it to any work of modern Machinima, you will quickly see what I am talking about. For me shows like "Daria", "Beavis and Butthead", "Simpsons", "Toy Story", "Home Movies", "Dr. Katz" or early Transformers episodes (anything up until and including the 1986 animated film) and King of the Hill made a lasting impression on me. I know that besides Toy Story they are all more or less 2D animated pieces but in my mind we often lose what was great with a previous technology when we move to a new one.

For example, prior to working in the technology sector (and 3D Modeling) I worked at Quad Recording Studios in Manhattan (www.quadnyc.com) and was an assistant audio engineer. Now in that field, it took a long time before the practices that dominated the analog recording industry translated to digital recording; digital recording provided some distinct advantages, but their true benefits weren't leveraged until what was great about analog recording was grafted into digital recording. Until then working with the new technology had a net negative effect on the work at hand, and I see the same thing happening with the explosion and proliferation of 3D modeling and animation technology.

Remember that we are already animated. If we could perfectly recreate our motions, colors, and textures so that the viewer is unaware that they are viewing animation, that would be cool, yes. It would even be incredibly useful for realistic video games, or to reduce production costs of live action films by being able to animate the next Peter Jackson film without anyone knowing they were seeing animation. However, this would not elevate the art form of Projected Animation. Nor is this a realistic or desirable goal in my mind, since nothing beats live action footage like actual live action footage if that is what you are going for. The idea that we are going to have compelling animated features or series in the style of the latest "Call of Duty" game is misguided and is not driven by animators as much as by the casual fanboy community and video game producers.

In my mind, animation is about stepping out of your world and into a representative (more than realistic) piece of moving art. The unreal but bright coloring of "The Simpsons" and "Beavis and Butthead" is intoxicating as are their surreal movements and expressions. We want to relate to the content we consume but we don't want to watch video footage of the real world when we want to escape into an animated world, so why is everyone moving in that direction? Well like so many things, people tend to immediately embrace new technology without giving consideration to its inherent value or its best use. The same thing happened with digital recording technology in the 1980's (but by the turn of the millennium engineers knew how to wield it in such a way that fully capitalized on its strengths).

So let's get together and create a package around the Blender suite that gives the animator the ability to have real time controls of their models; let's create a tool set where we can key map any point to any key on the keyboard and provide a means of control; let's create sets of controls useful for different circumstances (increased face controls for when our avatars are in a seated position for example). Bottom line: lets merge what is great about Machinima with what is great about Projected Animation Art.

People have played with the term "Digital Puppetry", but let's master it and put Blender on top of the heap when it comes to Machinima and more importantly low cost, quick, and most importantly, *expressive* animation.

I think that beyond reducing cost and hassle, we will accomplish two important things. First, we will really create a new form of PAA that will have its own characteristics (possibly getting closer to what is in your head in the time you have to accomplish that difficult feat). Secondly, we may be able to make production quality animation truly accessible to the masses. Machinima to date has not accomplished the latter. I could rattle off the name of a few Machinist series, but none of them can compare to the list I gave earlier of what touched me growing up. None of them can be confused with what has been put out by professional animators in the past half century.

I am less concerned with the "democratizing" effect to be honest, because our shop is linked with a great studio that goes by the name Fulcrum Films and we have multiple animated projects that we need this tool set for (as I'm sure you have projects you would like to quickly animate). Making this work for that shop would be enough for me personally, but bringing a new form of PAA to the world would be all the better.

To be clear too, we are not aiming at taking the time and care away from modeling or texturing or any such thing. Only the art of actually animating are we looking to tackle. So many tools have cropped up to aid in modeling (like Sculpting, model marketplaces, etc) that we feel our time is best spent giving control to the animator over the actual animation (and not doing this using a mimicry approach as in MoCap or the "Scanner Darkly" methods).

We are going to become masters of the Blender Game Engine for non-gaming uses. If we are not satisfied with the BGE then we will model in Blender and migrate to Unity. We believe in this approach and we will accomplish it. We are asking for what help we can get so we can all benefit from our findings, so please contact us if you are interested in helping (either monetarily or with time and technical assistance). We are currently going under the project code name "Puppet Smoothie" to denote the connection to digital puppetry, and of course the literal use of the term "Blender".

If our goal isn't clear at this point let me put it another way. There is a documentary called "6 Days to Air" in which they document the writing, sketching, animating and airing of an episode of South Park. Astoundingly this all takes place within a 6 day period (more or less). Now the fact that this *can happen at all* is a feat of modern technology and a credit to the animators in that particular studio. That said, the large staff, the years of animating experience needed, the considerable budget available, and the (let's be honest) crack-head levels of caffeine needed to accomplish this is nothing to be sniffed at. What we want is to be able to accomplish is this same incredible feat with a much smaller staff and budget (2 to 4 people max). Not only that but we would like the option to present in 3D, in 2D (South Park is of course a very rough example of 2D), or some merged format (like recent Simpsons or the approaches that make 3D look like it is made with brush strokes on a 2D-ish flattened background).

It is not hard to see how incredibly useful this would be. It would not really reduce the time in creating the *first* episode of a series per se (because all the models and backdrops need to be created and such), but it would **drastically reduce the cost of future episodes** – especially for series that take place in a limited number of places such as "Dr. Katz" or even "Beavis and Butthead". With regard to model creation, there really have been incredible strides that have already reduced the workflow and production costs associated with it. Again getting there is not going to be a simple feat, so let us know if you would like to help out. We have not decided if this will be an Open Source project or not but anyone helping out will get to use the finished product for sure. We are anxious to have this tool set at our disposal.

In fact, at Fulcrum Films (of which I am also a stakeholder) they have a few series planned where all of the action will take place in one of three settings (at least for the first six episodes) so this would be perfect for them. I'm sure there are many other film, tv and new media companies out there that share this same desire.

If you think about this, it's essentially like having the animated characters as real actors at your disposal and simple taking multiple "takes" until you get their "performances" down right. Now I did a lot of dogging of conventional Machinima in this chapter but let's not miss the **current major wins of Machinima** that we want to retain:

1. You can animate in real time by controlling an avatar.
2. Your avatar can have interactions with objects in its environment that are based on the rules of the game engine, and therefore you don't need to specifically animate.
3. If a scene has multiple principles you can retain the real time component by having multiple users (players/animators/etc.) each controlling their respective avatars and can interact with others in real time.
4. In some environments the camera work can be added also in real time.
5. Once your environment, objects, and avatars are created/colored/dressed/etc. future episodic work is just a

matter of performances, camera work and editing.

These are some hefty wins already. Thousands upon thousands of machinists are satisfied with just the above, and you can see why. All we are planning on doing is retaining much of the above, but **we will be adding the following abilities**:

1. Break through the restraints inherent in any given game environment by making it easier to interact with the game engine. In practical terms this will likely manifest primarily in features like key mapping where **keyboard letters can be assigned to** certain movements or better yet, **points in your rig that you can "grab"** by pressing those keys and then have another set of controls dictate their movements (again for use in real time animation).

2. Gain easy **control of the camera in real time** (either during the animation phase or manipulated during replay) so we can do professional style camera work including tracking shots, crane shots and racking focus with greater ease.

3. **Advanced facial controls** so that you can full control of expression (something more-or-less absent in iClone, MovieStorm, and definitely Second Life).

4. **Viability for Production Quality work.** Not sort-of professional, I want something ready for Cartoon Networks Adult Swim line up, something that stacks up with "Home Movies", the newer "Beavis and Butthead" episodes (that rely more on CGI), etc. We don't just want to win Machinima contests here.

5. Do everything in our power to eliminate the **video game feel,** even though we will be essentially be operating a Blender game produced with its BGE.

6. **Be able to accomplish a complete animated episode in 6 days flat** (without the benefit of large budgets or a full staff of dedicated animators) and have the quality be on par with South Park. **Not *like* South Park but I guess the 3D equivalent.** We are not trying to be able to produce 22 minutes worth of Sintel quality footage (for Blender fans familiar with that incredible Open Source Movie). But if we can just create expressive characters that don't look like they're in a video game, and look at least as good as "Home

Movies" or "South Park" then even that is going to be extremely valuable.

Again, we are not trying to directly recreate the 2D work of yesteryear. Rather, we are going to stylistically take a step back from trying to recreate a faithful recreation of the world we live in and embrace the colorful and representative approach, so that we will be more in the ball park of "Daria" and "Beavis and Butthead" and less like we are playing "Battlefield 3" or watching the 2007 animated version of "Beowulf". Again that is our personal approach and much of what we develop will translate to models and environments that are crafted more in the school of realism (if you prefer that approach).

Regardless of your artistic preference you should be able to appreciate the immense value that would come from accomplishing our six directives listed out above. If you want to be a part of this, please contact us and tell us a little about yourself and your interest. We could very well be the small band of pioneers that change the face of projected animation forever!

Email: filmfulcrum@gmail.com

Justin Valencia and Jordan Robert Kaufman

CONCLUSION

For both of us it has been an absolute pleasure writing this volume. I hope that we have gotten you excited about using Blender and extending it with Python. I hope you are starting to see the power of Blender and of gaining access to its internal workings using its API. Also, we hope that you will deepen your skills beyond this volume and join us in our Puppet Smoothie project so that we can perfect expressive digital puppetry and give new meaning to the word: Machinima.

We are planning more volumes in the future. Obviously when we are successful with Puppet Smoothie, we will wrap the project in a volume on the subject. The complexity of that project would be a large jump from this volume, so we may do a middle volume to get scriptures more comfortable with manipulating meshes and even logic bricks within Python. This will be critical as part of Puppet Smoothie, so we might as well document it so others can leverage our work. It may be a difficult journey but our destination will make it all worth it.

We view it as a super power that we are trying to attain. People normally think of flying or superhuman strength when they think of super powers. I for one would be more than satisfied with the super power of being able to deliver a production grade episode of animation within a week with minimal assistance and budget. Also, being able to give that super power to junior animators and see the production side of Level Development scale to take on multiple animation projects at once and become a fully-fledged animation studio, all the while doing it for a fraction of the cost, and then helping other studios join in all the fun is going to be beyond words. All I can say is: JOIN US!

Justin Valencia and Jordan Robert Kaufman

76

GO FIGURES

Justin Valencia and Jordan Robert Kaufman

INDEX

I hope you enjoy the index that follows. In addition to being useful, I've tried to include any fun references that are made throughout the body of the text. Enjoy!

P

PAA · 66, 67, 69, 70
Python · i, 1, 2, 5, 6, 9, 13, 14, 15, 19, 20, 23, 26, 27, 32, 77, 84

Q

Quad Recording · 68

R

register_class · 28, 29
Roland Hess · 60

S

Scanner Darkly · 64, 65, 70
Spider-Man 2 · 15
SQL Server · 2, 8

T

The Secret of Kells · 15

W

Waking Life · 64, 66

ABOUT THE AUTHORS

Justin Valencia is an up and coming technology specialist and author that lives in Nevada with his supportive family. He loves to connect with other Blender, Python, SQL, and open source enthusiasts so feel free to send feedback to:
iwmsconsultant@gmail.com

Jordan Robert Kaufman has almost two decades of experience in technology centered primarily around IWMS software, Audio Engineering, and alternative animation techniques. He resides in the Las Vegas valley with his amazingly supportive wife, Jamie, and his daughter Abigail.
filmfulcrum@gmail.com
Twitter: @Jordan_RK